Delicious
AMISH RECIPES

Phyllis Pellman Good

People's Place Book No. 5

Good Books

Intercourse, PA 17534
800/762-7171
www.goodbks.com

Traditional Amish Table Prayer

Enable us to use Thy manifold blessings
    with moderation;
Grant our hearts wisdom to avoid excess
    in eating and drinking
    and in the cares of this life;
Teach us to put our trust in Thee
    and to await Thy helping hand.

—*Traditional Amish Table Prayer*

Design by Dawn J. Ranck

Cover Photographs: Background photo by Mark Wiens; Center photo by Kenneth Pellman.
Back Cover Photograph: Jonathan Charles

DELICIOUS AMISH RECIPES
Copyright © 1997 by Good Books, Intercourse, PA 17534
International Standard Book Number: 1-56148-227-7
Library of Congress Catalog Card Number: 97-34003

Library of Congress Cataloging-in-Publication Data

Good, Phyllis Pellman
    Delicious Amish recipes / Phyllis Pellman Good.
        p. cm. -- (People's Place book : no. 5)
    Includes index.
    ISBN: 1-56148-227-7
    1. Cookery, Amish. 2. Cookery--Pennsylvania. I. Title. II. Series: People's
Place booklet ; no. 5.
TX715.G61717   1997
641.5'66--dc21   97-34003
                                                                 CIP

Table of Contents

About These Recipes—

Amish families gather around their long kitchen tables for three meals together every day. It may be a routine, but the food they enjoy is beyond the ordinary.

The Amish dress austerely; they discipline themselves by driving buggies and refusing electricity in their homes. They work hard and long. But when they eat, they celebrate!

The Amish are friends of the earth, respectful of the soil, alert to the seasons. And so their gardens produce bountifully. Their abundant farms offer them eggs, milk, cream, and livestock.

And when they set aside work to socialize, the Amish surround their events with food—plentiful, homemade, and comfortingly delicious. The school picnic, sisters day, family reunions, farm auctions, singings and weddings and church— all would be unthinkable without a vast spread of food.

Here are some of their favorite recipes. Prepare them, eat them with family or friends, and sample one part of these people's lives.

These dishes are likely to become some of your favorites, too!
—Phyllis Pellman Good

Breads, Rolls, & Buns

Honey Oatmeal Bread

Makes 2-3 loaves

2 cups boiling water	1 egg
1 cup dry rolled oats	1 tsp. vinegar
2 Tbsp. yeast	2 Tbsp. blackstrap molasses
1/3 cup lukewarm water	2 cups whole wheat flour
1 Tbsp. salt	4-5 cups white flour
1/2 cup honey	

1. Pour boiling water over dry oats. Let stand 30 minutes. Meanwhile, dissolve yeast in lukewarm water.
2. To first mixture add the salt, honey, egg, vinegar, molasses, and yeast mixture. Gradually add enough flour so the dough can be kneaded. (Dough should be slightly sticky.) Knead 5-10 minutes.
3. Let rise until double in size, about 1 hour. Punch down, then divide into 2-3 loaves. Place in bread pans and let rise again.
4. Bake at 350° for 25-30 minutes.

Homemade White Bread

Makes 2 large or 3 medium loaves

1 pkg. dry yeast	1$^{1}/_{4}$ tsp. salt
1 tsp. sugar	$^{1}/_{3}$ cup sugar
$^{1}/_{2}$ cup lukewarm water	1$^{3}/_{4}$ Tbsp. shortening
2 cups lukewarm water	7-8 cups flour

1. Dissolve the yeast and sugar in $^{1}/_{2}$ cup lukewarm water.
2. Mix 2 cups water, salt, sugar, and shortening in a large bowl. Add the yeast mixture to it and, gradually, the flour. Knead until smooth and elastic.
3. Place in a greased bowl, cover, and set in a warm place to rise until double.
4. Punch down. Let rise again. Put into large loaf pans or three medium-sized ones. Let rise again until double.
5. Bake at 350° for $^{1}/_{2}$ hour.

Whole Wheat Bread

Makes 4 loaves

2 pkgs. dry yeast	$^{1}/_{2}$ cup honey
4 cups warm water	2 tsp. salt
$^{1}/_{2}$ cup soft margarine or butter	6 cups whole wheat flour
$^{1}/_{4}$ cup molasses	4 cups white flour

1. Dissolve yeast in warm water.
2. Combine margarine, molasses, honey, and salt in a large bowl. Mix well.
3. Add yeast mixture. Gradually add flour. Turn onto floured surface and knead until smooth.
4. Place in greased bowl and let rise until double. Punch down. Let

dough rest a few minutes.

5. Shape into 4 loaves. Place in greased bread pans. Let rise about 1 hour.
6. Bake at 375° for 35-40 minutes.

Raisin Bread

Makes 5 loaves

1 15-oz. box raisins	1/2 cup sugar
2 Tbsp. dry yeast	1 Tbsp. cinnamon
1 cup warm water	1 Tbsp. salt
2 cups warm milk	2 eggs, beaten
1/2 cup oil	8-10 cups flour

1. Soak raisins 3-4 hours, or overnight, in water deep enough to cover them. Drain.
2. Dissolve yeast in warm water.
3. Combine milk, oil, sugar, cinnamon, salt, and eggs. Beat well. Add yeast mixture and raisins.
4. Gradually add flour, stirring by hand. When dough becomes too stiff to stir, finish working in flour with hands.
5. Place dough in greased bowl. Cover and let rise in warm place about 1 hour. Punch down, knead, and let rise another hour. Divide dough into 5 portions and form loaves. Place in greased pans and let rise another hour.
6. Bake at 300° for 50-60 minutes.

Potato Doughnuts with Glaze and Potato Dinner Rolls

Makes about 3 dozen doughnuts or rolls

1 cup sugar	1^1/$_2$ tsp. salt
1 cups mashed potatoes	1^1/$_2$-2 pkgs. dry yeast
^{1}/$_2$ cup lard or shortening	1 cup warm water
3 eggs, beaten	5 cups flour

1. Mix together well the sugar, potatoes, lard, eggs, and salt.
2. Dissolve the yeast in 1 cup warm water; then add to the above mixture.
3. Stir in about 3 cups flour. Add the remaining 2 cups flour while kneading, kneading until the dough is no longer sticky but moist.
4. Let rise until doubled in a warm place.

For Potato Dinner Rolls

1. Roll out dough until it is ^{3}/$_4$"-1" thick. Cut into bun shapes with a jar or doughnut cutter (or clover leaf—or crescent-shaped cutter) and put on greased cookie sheets about 2 inches apart.
2. Let rise until puffy but not doubled (they should not be touching).
3. Brush with milk. Bake at 325° until lightly golden brown, about 12 minutes.

For Doughnuts

1. Roll out dough until it is ^{1}/$_2$" thick. Cut out with a doughnut cutter; then place on clean towels laid over cookie sheets or boards. Let rise until almost double.
2. Fry in oil, heated to 350° - 375° , about 4 inches deep. Keep oil at that temperature throughout the frying.
3. Turn doughnuts over once while frying, when they turn golden brown.

Doughnut Glaze

1 lb. 10x sugar
1/2 cup rich milk (or a bit more)

1 Tbsp. soft butter
1 tsp. vanilla

Heat together just until butter is melted and milk is warm, stirring until smooth. Glaze while doughnuts are hot.

Cinnamon Flop

Makes 2 9" pans

1 cup sugar
2 cups flour
2 tsp. baking powder
1 Tbsp. melted butter

1 cup milk
brown sugar, cinnamon,
 and butter for top

1. Sift sugar, flour, and baking powder together.
2. Add butter and milk and stir until well blended.
3. Divide mixture between 2 well greased 9" pie or cake pans.
4. Sprinkle tops with flour, then brown sugar, then cinnamon. Push chunks of butter into the dough. This makes holes and later makes the cake gooey as it bakes.
5. Bake at 350° for 30 minutes.

Mamie Fisher's Cinnamon Rolls

Makes 4 dozen rolls

1/2 cup sugar
1/2 cup shortening
1 1/2 tsp. salt
1 cup milk
1 cup lukewarm water

2 pkgs. dry yeast
2 eggs, beaten
1/2 tsp. nutmeg (optional)
7 cups flour

Filling
6 Tbsp. melted butter
1 1/2 cups brown sugar

1 Tbsp. cinnamon
1 cup raisins (optional)

1. In large bowl, combine 1/2 cup sugar, shortening, and salt. Scald milk and pour over shortening mixture.
2. Combine yeast and warm water and set aside to dissolve.
3. When milk mixture has cooled, add beaten eggs, dissolved yeast, and nutmeg. Beat well.
4. Gradually add flour, beating well. Turn onto floured surface and knead lightly, adding only enough flour so dough can be handled. Place in greased bowl. Cover and let rise in warm place until double (about 2 hours).
5. Divide dough in half. Roll each piece into a rectangle about 1/4" thick. Brush with melted butter and sprinkle with mixture of brown sugar and cinnamon. Sprinkle with raisins. Roll up like a jelly roll and cut slices 1/2" thick.
6. Place slices 1" apart in greased baking pans. Let rise about 1 hour.
7. Bake at 375° for 20 minutes.

Pecan Sticky Buns

Makes 2 dozen buns

1 pkg. dry yeast	3^1/$_4$-4 cups flour
^{1}/$_4$ cup warm water	^{1}/$_2$ cup pecans
^{1}/$_4$ cup shortening	^{1}/$_2$ cup brown sugar
^{1}/$_4$ cup sugar	^{1}/$_4$ cup butter or margarine
1 cup milk, scalded,	1 Tbsp. light corn syrup
or 1 cup warm water	butter
1 tsp. salt	^{1}/$_4$ cup brown sugar
1 egg, beaten	1 tsp. cinnamon

1. Dissolve yeast in warm water.
2. In large bowl, cream shortening and sugar together. Pour hot milk or water over mixture. Cool to lukewarm. Add salt and 1 cup flour and beat well. Beat in yeast mixture and egg.
3. Gradually add remaining flour to form a soft dough, beating well.
4. Brush top of dough with softened margarine or butter. Cover and let rise in warm place until double (1^1/$_2$-2 hours).
5. While dough is rising, divide pecans between two greased 9^1/$_2$ x 5 x 3 pans. Make syrup by slowly heating together ^{1}/$_2$ cup brown sugar, ^{1}/$_4$ cup butter or margarine, and 1 Tbsp. light corn syrup. Pour half of syrup over each pan of pecans.
6. Punch down dough and knead slightly.
7. Divide dough in half. Roll each half into a rectangle, approximately 12" x 8." Spread with butter and sprinkle with a mixture of ^{1}/$_4$ cup brown sugar and 1 tsp. cinnamon.
8. Roll into a jelly roll. Cut into 1-1^1/$_2$" slices. Place rolls on top of pecans and syrup, about ^{3}/$_4$" apart.
9. Let rise until double and then bake at 375° for about 25 minutes.
10. Remove from oven and turn pan upside down onto a flat plate. Syrup will run down through the rolls, and pecans will be on top.

Pumpkin Bread

2 full-sized loaves, or 3 1-lb. coffee can-shaped loaves

3 cups sugar
1 cup oil
4 eggs
1 tsp. nutmeg
1 tsp. cinnamon
1^1/$_2$ tsp. salt

2 cups pumpkin,
    cooked and mashed
^{2}/$_3$ cup water
1 tsp. baking soda
^{1}/$_2$ tsp. baking powder
3 cups flour

1. Combine sugar, oil, eggs, nutmeg, cinnamon, and salt. Beat well.
2. Add remaining ingredients and mix well.
3. Pour batter into 2 well greased loaf pans or 3 1-lb. coffee cans. Bake at 350° for 1 hour.
4. Slide bread out of pans or cans and cool.

Variations:
1. Add 2 cups chopped pecans to batter.
2. Add ^{2}/$_3$ cup raisins to batter.

Homemade Zucchini Bread

Makes 2 loaves

3 eggs
2 cups sugar
2 cups zucchini, shredded
1 cup cooking oil
2 tsp. vanilla
3 cups flour
1 tsp. salt

1 tsp. baking soda
1 tsp. baking powder
2 tsp. cinnamon
^{1}/$_2$ tsp. nutmeg
^{1}/$_4$ tsp. cloves
^{1}/$_2$ cup chopped nuts
^{1}/$_2$ cup raisins (optional)

1. Beat eggs till foamy. Stir in sugar, zucchini, oil, and vanilla.
2. Gradually add dry ingredients and spices. Stir in nuts and raisins, if desired.
3. Pour into bread pans which have been greased only on the bottoms. Bake at 325° for 60-80 minutes.
4. Cool 10 minutes. Remove from pans and cool completely. Use this as bread, or frost it and serve for dessert.

Soft Pretzels
Makes 12 pretzels

1¹/2 cups warm water	¹/4 cup baking soda
2 pkgs. dry yeast	1 cup cool water
¹/2 tsp. salt	shortening
4¹/2 cups flour	salt (table or coarse)

1. Stir yeast into warm water. When dissolved, stir in salt and up to 3¹/2 cups flour.
2. Knead in the remaining flour. When dough is smooth and elastic, return to bowl and let rise in warm place for 15 minutes.
3. Tear dough into 12 equal pieces. Roll each piece into a rope, about 8-10 inches long.
4. Put 1 cup cool water in bowl. Stir baking soda into water until dissolved. Soak each rope, one by one, in the water-soda mixture for 2 minutes each.
5. Remove from water and shape each into a pretzel.
6. Place pretzels on greased cookie sheets and sprinkle them with either coarse or table salt.
7. Bake for 20 minutes at 350°. Serve warm.

Soups

Chicken Corn Rivel Soup

Makes 8-10 servings

3-4 lb. stewing chicken
2 Tbsp. salt
$1/4$ tsp. pepper
$1^1/2$ cups celery, chopped
1 medium onion, chopped

2 Tbsp. minced parsley
1 quart corn
  (fresh, frozen, or canned)
rivels
hard-cooked egg or parsley

1. In large kettle cover chicken with water. Add salt and pepper. Cook until soft. Remove bones and skin from chicken and cut meat into small pieces.
2. Heat broth to boiling point and add remaining ingredients. Cook about 15 minutes. Add meat. Heat thoroughly. Garnish with hard-cooked egg or parsley.

Rivels

1 cup flour
1 egg

$1/4$ cup milk

1. Combine flour and egg. Add milk.
2. Mix rivels by cutting ingredients together with two forks to make crumbs the size of cherry stones. Drop rivels into boiling broth while stirring continually to prevent rivels from packing together.

Beef Vegetable Soup

Makes 12-14 servings

1 beef soup bone	2 cups peas
1¹/₂ tsp. salt	2 cups green beans
2 quarts water	2 cups lima beans
2 cups potatoes, peeled and diced	2 cups corn
2 cups carrots, sliced	2 cups tomato juice
1 cup celery, chopped	¹/₂ cup rice
1 cup cabbage, shredded	

1. Cook soup bone and salt in water until meat is tender. Remove from broth, take meat from bone, and cut into small pieces. Set meat aside.
2. Add first four vegetables and cook until tender.
3. Add remaining ingredients and cook until all vegetables are soft. Stir in meat and serve.

Hamburger Vegetable Soup

Makes 4-6 servings

2 Tbsp. butter	¹/₂ cup celery, chopped
1 onion, chopped	1 cup potatoes, diced
1 lb. hamburger	2 cups tomato juice
1¹/₂ tsp. salt	2 cups milk
1 cup carrots, diced	¹/₄ cup flour

1. Brown meat and onion in butter. Add remaining ingredients except milk and flour and cook until vegetables are tender.
2. Combine milk and flour and stir until smooth. Add to soup and cook until thickened.

Split Pea with Ham Soup

Makes 6-8 servings

1 lb. dried split peas
2 qts. water
1 ham hock
1 cup celery, finely chopped

1 medium onion, finely chopped
2 carrots,
   finely chopped or shredded
salt and pepper to taste

1. Combine peas and water. Bring to a boil and boil 2 minutes. Remove from heat. Cover and let set for 1 hour.
2. Add remaining ingredients. Bring to boiling point. Reduce heat and simmer 2$^1/_2$-3 hours until peas look creamed and ham hock is tender.
3. Remove ham hock. Trim meat from bone and dice. Return meat to soup. Heat thoroughly and serve.
4. Add water or milk to soup if you want a thinner consistency.

Amish Bean Soup

Makes 6-8 servings

1 cup navy beans, cooked
$^1/_4$ cup water
salt and pepper
3 quarts milk

about $^1/_2$ loaf stale bread,
   torn into bite-sized pieces
2-3 Tbsp. butter or margarine,
   browned

1. Bring cooked beans and water to boil in soup pan. Add seasonings to taste.
2. Pour in milk and bring to boiling point.
3. Stir in bread. Pour browned butter over (see page 33). Serve immediately.

To cook dried navy beans:
1. Soak for 8 hours overnight in water (4 cups water to 1 cup dried beans).

2. Bring beans to boil in soaking water. Cover. Simmer for approximately 3 hours or longer, if desired.

Potato Soup with Eggs

Makes 6 servings

3-4 potatoes, peeled and diced
1/4 cup celery, chopped
1 1/2 cups water
2 Tbsp. butter or margarine

1 quart milk
1 Tbsp. parsley
salt and pepper to taste
2 hard-cooked eggs, diced

1. Cook the potatoes and celery in the water and butter until tender.
2. Add the milk, seasonings, and egg and heat thoroughly.

Cream of Tomato Soup

Makes 4-6 servings

2 cups tomato juice
  (home-canned with peppers,
  onions, and celery)
1/2 tsp. baking soda

1 quart milk
1 tsp. salt
dash of pepper
2 Tbsp. butter

1. Heat tomato juice to boiling. When boiling, add baking soda and stir quickly because mixture will foam. Remove from heat.
2. Meanwhile, heat milk. Do not boil. Add salt, pepper, and butter. When milk is hot, add tomato mixture to it. Serve soup with crackers.

Broccoli Cheddar Chowder

Makes 8 servings

1¹/4 lbs. broccoli
4 Tbsp. butter
¹/4 cup mushrooms, chopped
1 Tbsp. onion, chopped

4 Tbsp. flour
3¹/2 cups milk
1 lb. sharp cheddar cheese, grated
1 tsp. salt

1. Cook broccoli. Chop and set aside.
2. Melt butter in large, heavy pan. Add mushrooms and onion. Saute until tender.
3. Add flour and stir until bubbly.
4. Gradually add 1¹/2 cups milk, stirring constantly to prevent lumps. Add cheese and stir until smooth. Add remaining milk.
5. Add broccoli and heat thoroughly.

Cream of Cauliflower Soup

Makes 4 servings

4 cups cauliflower
¹/2 cup water
1 tsp. salt
¹/2 tsp. dried basil

2 Tbsp. butter
2¹/2 Tbsp. flour
3 cups milk

1. In saucepan combine cauliflower, water, salt, and basil. Cook cauliflower until tender.
2. In separate pan melt butter until lightly browned. Add flour and stir until smooth. Gradually add milk, stirring constantly until thickened. Pour over vegetable mixture and stir until blended. Heat through and serve.

Stewed Crackers

Makes 4-5 servings

1/4-1/2 lb. (about 50-60)
  buttermilk, saltine,
  or round soup crackers

2 1/2 cups milk
2 Tbsp. butter or margarine
3/4 cup milk

1. Butter the bottom and sides of a 1 1/2-quart casserole. Lay dry crackers in the casserole.
2. Heat 2 1/2 cups milk to scalding. Pour over crackers. Cover casserole and let stand at least 5 minutes, checking once to make sure the crackers are in the milk.
3. Just before serving, heat the butter until browned. Add 3/4 cup milk to butter and warm it.
4. Pour browned butter and 3/4 cup milk over crackers. Serve.

Cold Milk Soup

1 serving

1 slice bread
1 cup fresh fruit,
  sliced and sweetened

1 cup cold milk

1. Crumble bread into soup bowl.
2. Dish fruit over top. Sprinkle with sugar if the fruit is not sweetened.
3. Cover with milk. ("It's best when the fruit and milk are really cold!")

Salads

Cutting Lettuce with Dressing
Makes 4 servings

a serving bowlful,
　　or half a dishpan full,
　　of cutting lettuce
2 Tbsp. cider vinegar

2 Tbsp. sugar
$3/4$ cup cream
3 hard-cooked eggs, diced
dash of paprika

1. Wash and drain lettuce well.
2. Mix vinegar and sugar; then add cream and blend.
3. Pour over lettuce.
4. Garnish with diced egg and sprinkles of paprika.

Layered Fresh Vegetable Salad
Makes 18-20 servings

1 medium head of lettuce,
　　torn into bite-sized pieces
1 cup celery, diced
4 hard-cooked eggs, sliced
10 oz. frozen peas,
　　uncooked and separated
$1/2$ cup green pepper, diced

1 onion, sliced thin
$1^1/2$ cups mayonnaise
2 Tbsp. sugar
4 oz. cheddar cheese, grated
8 slices bacon, fried
　　and crumbled
parsley

1. In large bowl layer lettuce, followed by celery, eggs, peas, pepper, and onion.
2. Combine mayonnaise and sugar and spread over vegetables. Sprinkle with cheese.
3. Cover and refrigerate 8-12 hours.
4. Sprinkle with crumbled bacon and parsley just before serving. To serve, toss the salad, or serve it layered as prepared.

Wilted Dandelion Greens with Hot Bacon Dressing

Makes 4 servings

a large bowlful of young dandelion shoots (or endive, romaine lettuce, or spinach)	1 Tbsp. vinegar
	1 Tbsp. flour
	1^1/$_2$ Tbsp. sugar
6 slices bacon	^{1}/$_4$-^{1}/$_2$ cup water

1. Pull the dandelion leaves off their stalks and chop the leaves. Drop them into a pot of boiling water. Let stand for 5 to 10 minutes. Drain leaves, pouring off juice.
2. Brown the bacon. Remove from drippings and crumble. Set aside. Add vinegar, flour, sugar, and water to drippings. Cook until thickened. Stir in bacon.
3. Pour warm dressing over wilted dandelion and serve.

Broccoli Salad

Makes 10-12 servings

2 bunches of broccoli,
   cut in bite-sized pieces
2 medium red onions, sliced thin
1/4 cup raisins

8 slices bacon, fried and crumbled
1 cup mayonnaise
1/4 cup sugar
2 Tbsp. vinegar

1. Mix broccoli, onions, raisins, and bacon together gently.
2. Blend mayonnaise, sugar, and vinegar thoroughly.
3. Fold dressing into vegetable mixture and refrigerate 1 to 2 hours before serving.

Variations:
1. Sprinkle finished salad with 1 cup shredded cheese.
2. Add 1/2 lb. fresh, sliced mushrooms to salad.
3. Substitute 1/2 cup shredded purple cabbage in place of onions.

Cole Slaw

Makes 6 servings

3 cups cabbage, shredded

Variation:
Shred one small carrot and chop half of a green pepper. Blend with cabbage to add flavor and color.

Dressing 1:
1/3 cup sweet or sour cream
2 Tbsp. sugar

2 Tbsp. apple cider vinegar
1/2 tsp. salt

1. Mix together dressing ingredients until smooth.
2. Fold into shredded cabbage. Cool and serve.

Dressing 2:
3/4 cup sugar
1/4 cup vinegar

1/2 tsp. salt
2 Tbsp. water

1. Mix together until smooth.
2. Fold into shredded cabbage. Cool and serve.

Cucumbers and Onions

Makes 4-6 servings

2 medium cucumbers
2 medium onions
salt

2-3 Tbsp. mayonnaise
1 Tbsp. sugar
1 Tbsp. vinegar

1. Peel cucumbers and slice thin. Layer in shallow dish, sprinkling each layer with salt. Let stand overnight.
2. In the morning, drain cucumbers and rinse. Let dry on paper towels.
3. Slice onions thin. Mix gently with cucumber slices.
4. Beat together the mayonnaise, sugar, and vinegar until creamy. Stir into mixed cucumbers and onions.

   The dressing should be plentiful so the salad is creamy. Increase amounts of dressing ingredients, proportionally, if needed.

Macaroni Salad

Makes 20 servings

1 lb. macaroni (or baby seashells)
1¹/₂ cups celery, chopped
¹/₂ cup carrots, finely grated

¹/₄ cup onion, finely chopped
6 hard-cooked eggs, sliced
paprika

1. Cook macaroni as directed, drain, and cool.
2. Set aside 1 hard-cooked egg; then stir together gently the cooked macaroni, celery, carrots, onion, and remaining eggs.

Dressing:
1 pint salad dressing
¹/₄ cup vinegar

³/₄ cup sugar
2 Tbsp. prepared mustard

1. Blend together; then fold into macaroni salad mixture.
2. Garnish with 1 hard-cooked egg and paprika.

Potato Salad

Makes 10 servings

6 medium-sized potatoes
1 small onion, chopped fine
1 cup celery, chopped

1 tsp. celery seed
1 tsp. salt
4 hard-cooked eggs, diced

1. Cook potatoes in their jackets until soft. Peel and dice.
2. Mix potatoes gently with the remaining five ingredients; then add to the dressing.

Dressing:

2 eggs, well beaten
3/4 cup sugar
1 tsp. cornstarch
salt to taste
1/4-1/2 cup vinegar

1/2 cup cream or evaporated milk
1 tsp. mustard
3 Tbsp. butter, softened
1 cup mayonnaise

1. Mix eggs with sugar, cornstarch, and salt. Add vinegar, cream, and mustard. Cook until thickened.
2. Remove from heat and beat in butter. Add mayonnaise and mix until smooth.
3. Add potato mixture to the cooled dressing, folding gently together.

Apple Salad

Makes 10 servings

8 unpeeled apples, diced
1/2 cup celery, chopped
1/2 cup raisins

1/2 cup broken walnuts
1 cup miniature marshmallows
  (optional)

Stir above ingredients together, gently.

Dressing:

1 Tbsp. cornstarch
1 cup water
1 tsp. vinegar
1/4 tsp. salt

1/2 cup sugar
1/4 cup rich milk or cream
1 tsp. vanilla

1. Blend cornstarch into water. Stir in other ingredients over low heat until all are dissolved. Bring to boiling point.
2. Cool and pour over apple mixture. Chill. Garnish with parsley to serve.

Stewed Apples

2 quarts apples   **1¹/₂-2 cups raisins**
¹/₃-¹/₂ cup sugar

1. Core and quarter apples. Peel them if you like. Add sugar according to taste and the sweetness of the apples and raisins.
2. Pour into a saucepan and add an inch or two of water. Add raisins to taste.
3. Cook *slowly,* stirring up frequently, only until the "rawness is broken down. Then stop!"

Applesauce

5 lbs. ripe apples   **1-1¹/₂ cups sugar**
3 cups water

1. Cut apples in half and core. Remove any spots; then cut apples into quarters.
2. Put apples in deep, heavy saucepan. Add water and cook. Stir occasionally to keep fruit cooking evenly throughout and to prevent apples from sticking.
3. When apples are thoroughly soft, pour into food press, standing in a large pan. Press apples through sieve and stir in sugar (lesser amount initially) while sauce is still warm so sugar dissolves. Taste. Add more sugar if needed.
4. Allow to cool and serve, or pour into canning jars while still hot and process.

Carrot and Pineapple Salad

Makes 6 servings

3-oz. pkg. orange gelatin
1/2 tsp. salt
1 cup boiling water
1 cup cold pineapple juice

1 Tbsp. lemon juice or vinegar
1 cup crushed pineapple, drained
1 cup carrots, coarsely grated

1. Dissolve gelatin and salt in boiling water. Add pineapple juice and lemon juice.
2. Refrigerate until mixture begins to jell.
3. Fold in crushed pineapple and carrots. Return to refrigerator until fully jelled.
3. Cut into squares and serve each piece on a lettuce leaf.

Cranberry Fruit Mold

Makes 8 servings

3-oz. pkg. cherry or
    strawberry gelatin
1 cup hot water
1/2 cup cold water
1/2 lb. cranberries

3 apples
2 oranges, or 1/2 cup crushed
    pineapple, drained
1/4 cup nuts, chopped
3/4 cup sugar

1. Dissolve gelatin in hot water; then add cold water; Cool mixture and set aside until beginning to thicken.
2. Wash and grind cranberries. Pare and chop apples into small chunks.
3. Stir together ground cranberries, chopped apples, oranges (or pineapple), nuts, and sugar.
4. Add to slightly thickened gelatin mixture; then pour into a mold and chill until salad is firm and holds its shape. Unmold on salad greens.

Spiced Cantaloupe

2 lbs. ripe firm cantaloupe
3 cups water
1^1/$_2$ cups apple cider vinegar
2^1/$_4$ cups sugar

^{1}/$_2$ tsp. salt
^{1}/$_4$ tsp. oil of cinnamon
^{1}/$_4$ tsp. oil of cloves

1. Peel cantaloupe, remove seeds, and cut into chunks. Pack gently into sterilized pint jars.
2. Combine remaining ingredients and bring to a boil. Let cool to room temperature.
3. Pour syrup into jars of cantaloupe, filling to 1" from top. Place self-sealing lid and screw ring on each jar. Place jars in home canner, bring water to boil, and boil for 15 minutes.

Chow Chow

2 quarts and 1 pint raw cauliflower
3 pints raw carrots
2 quarts and 1 pint celery
3^1/$_2$ pints raw green and red peppers

2^1/$_2$ pints raw baby lima beans
3 pints pickles
1 heaping quart raw onions
salt to taste

1. Dice each vegetable into ^{1}/$_2$-1" chunks.
2. Cook each vegetable separately. Season each with salt.
3. Drain (reserve juice from cooking celery) and gently mix all vegetables together.

Syrup:

1^1/$_2$ pints vinegar or more
1 pint juice from cooked celery
5^1/$_2$ lbs. sugar
6 oz. prepared mustard
3 Tbsp. mustard seed

2 tsp. turmeric
1 tsp. celery seed
2 Tbsp. cornstarch mixed
   with 1 tsp. water

1. Combine all ingredients. Add the mixed vegetables and heat to the boiling point.
2. Put in canning jars and seal.

Corn Relish

Makes about 6 pints

2 quarts corn kernels	4 cups apple cider vinegar
1 quart cabbage, chopped	1 cup water
1 cup sweet red peppers, chopped	1 tsp. celery seed
1 cup sweet green peppers, chopped	1 tsp. mustard seed
1 cup onions, diced	1 Tbsp. salt
2 cup onions, diced	1 tsp. turmeric
2 cups granulated sugar	1 tsp. dry mustard

1. Cook corn on cobs submerged in boiling water for 5 minutes. Plunge into cold water to stop cooking and preserve color. Drain, then cut corn from cobs.
2. Mix all vegetables together gently.
3. Combine sugar, vinegar, water, and spices (making sure sugar is dissolved). Pour over vegetables and simmer for 20 minutes, or until vegetables are tender but not mushy.
4. Spoon into hot sterilized jars and seal.

Three-Bean Salad

Makes 12 servings

1 pint green beans, cooked
1 pint yellow wax beans, cooked
1 pint kidney beans,
   cooked and rinsed

1 purple onion, sliced thin
1/2 cup celery, diced
1/2 cup red or green pepper,
   diced

1. Drain all the beans well and mix together. Stir in onion, celery, and peppers.
2. Stir in dressing. Let stand several hours or overnight to allow the flavors to blend.

Dressing:

3/4 cup sugar
2/3 cup vinegar
1/3 cup salad oil

1 tsp. salt
1/4 tsp. pepper

Blend together thoroughly; then pour over vegetables.

Pickled Red Beets

20 medium-size red beets
2 1/2 cups vinegar
2 1/2 cups beet juice
1 cup sugar

2 tsp. salt
10 whole cloves
2 cinnamon sticks

1. Scrub beets and remove tops. Cook beets until tender. Drain and reserve beet juice. Remove skins and cut beets into chunks.
2. Combine vinegar, juice, sugar, and spices. Bring to a boil. Remove spices. Add beet chunks and boil again. Pour into jars and seal.

Red Beet Eggs

6 hard-cooked eggs, peeled
2¹/₂ cups leftover red beet juice syrup

Pour cool syrup over cooked and peeled eggs. Let stand overnight. To serve, slice the eggs in half, lengthwise.

Seven Day Sweet Pickles

Makes about 7 pints

7 lbs. medium-size cucumbers
(about 3" long)
boiling water
1 quart apple cider vinegar

8 cups sugar
2 Tbsp. salt
2 Tbsp. mixed pickling spices

1. Scrub the pickles, put them in a large dishpan or crock, and cover them with boiling water. Let stand for 24 hours.
2. On day 2 drain them; then cover them again with fresh boiling water.
3. Repeat that process on days 3 and 4.
4. On day 5 drain the pickles, then cut them into ¹/₄" slices. Combine the vinegar, sugar, and seasonings and bring to a boil. Pour over sliced pickles.
5. On day 6 drain the syrup into a saucepan, bring it to a boil, and pour over the pickles once again.
6. Repeat that process on day 7; then spoon the pickles and syrup into hot sterilized jars and seal.

Vegetable Sandwich Spread

3 cups cucumbers
2 cups onions
1¹/2 red sweet peppers
1¹/2 green peppers
1/4 cup salt
1 cup apple cider vinegar
1/4 cup butter or margarine

1^1/2 cups sugar
1^1/2 Tbsp. flour
2 eggs, beaten
1/2 tsp. mustard seed
1/2 tsp. celery seed
1/2 cup cream

1. Grind cucumbers, onions, and red and green sweet peppers until fine. Mix salt thoroughly with vegetables. Let set for 2 hours.
2. Mix salted vegetables and vinegar in a saucepan and bring to a boil. Drain (reserving stock) and press until dry.
3. Blend butter or margarine, sugar, flour, eggs, spices, and reserved stock. Stir in vegetables and simmer for 5 minutes. Add cream and bring mixture to a boil.
4. Pack into hot sterilized jars and seal.

Egg and Olive Salad

Makes 4 servings

6 hard-cooked eggs
1/4 tsp. salt
dash of pepper

1/2 tsp. prepared mustard
1/4 cup mayonnaise
1-2 Tbsp. chopped green olives

1. Cut up eggs into small chunks.
2. Fold in remaining ingredients. Chill.
3. Serve on bread or rolls with lettuce leaves.

Vegetables

Amish Wedding Potatoes
(otherwise known as Special Mashed Potatoes!)
Makes 6 servings

6 medium-size potatoes,
   peeled and cut in chunks
$1/2$-$3/4$ cup milk, scalded

$1/2$ tsp. salt
brown butter

1. Cook potatoes until very soft in small amount of water. Pour $1/2$ cup milk and salt into the saucepan with the potatoes.
2. With a manual potato ricer, immediately mash the potatoes by hand. Add additional milk if they seem too stiff.
3. Stop mashing at whatever stage you prefer—when the potatoes have been formed into noodle-like strands, or when they are as smooth as an electric mixer's end result. (The Amish, because they do not have electricity in their homes, mash their potatoes by hand.)
4. Cover with brown butter.

Brown Butter

This simply prepared delicacy adds an elegant, rich flavor to almost any vegetable dish.

Melt several tablespoons of butter in a saucepan, and then let the butter sit on the heat a bit longer until it begins to brown.

Watch it carefully. Brown butter can quickly become burned butter! When the butter is fully browned, pour it over cooked vegetables and serve.

Creamed New Potatoes and Peas

Makes 4-6 servings

| 12 small new potatoes | 1 tsp. salt |
| 3 cups fresh peas | brown butter or white sauce |

1. Cook potatoes in a small amount of water until almost soft.
2. Add peas and cook just until they and the potatoes are tender. Stir in salt.
3. Spoon into serving dish and pour brown butter (page 33) or white sauce over.

White Sauce

| 2 Tbsp. butter or margarine | 1^1/$_2$ cups milk |
| 1^1/$_2$ Tbsp. flour | |

1. Melt butter or margarine. Stir in flour to form paste.
2. Gradually add milk, stirring constantly over heat until smooth and thickened.

Variation:

This creamy White Sauce can be served over other cooked vegetables also; for example, asparagus, cabbage, and soybeans. Typically, an Old Order Amish cook would pour this over a dish of vegetables, and then top it all off with brown butter!

Home-Fried Potatoes

Makes 6 servings

6 medium-size potatoes	dash of pepper
3 Tbsp. lard, butter, or margarine	1 tsp. salt
2 eggs, beaten	

1. Cook potatoes until soft. Cool and skin.
2. Melt shortening in skillet. Slice potatoes and slide into skillet. Pour beaten eggs over and season.
3. Let potatoes brown until crispy edges form. Then turn over with metal spatula, allowing other edges to brown.

Variation:

Use only 4 or 5 potatoes. Begin by toasting 2 buttered slices of bread, torn in bite-sized pieces, in hot skillet. Then add potatoes and continue as above.

Whole Browned Potatoes

Makes 6 servings

6 medium-size potatoes   **salt and pepper**
2 Tbsp. or more butter or margarine

1. Peel potatoes and steam until tender.
2. Melt butter or margarine in heavy skillet. Add potatoes and brown, stirring occasionally so all sides brown.
3. Sprinkle with salt and pepper and serve.

Variation:

Add cooked potatoes to a roaster containing beef or pork, and let them brown during the last 45 minutes of the meat's baking time.

Potato Cakes

Makes 4-6 servings

2 cups leftover mashed potatoes
1 egg, beaten
1 Tbsp. flour, or more if
   the potatoes are thin

2 Tbsp. cream, or less
   if the potatoes are thin
1 Tbsp. onion, chopped fine
2-3 Tbsp. shortening

1. Mix together all ingredients except shortening.
2. Heat shortening. Drop potatoes by tablespoonsful into shortening and brown on both sides.

Creamy Scalloped Potatoes

Makes 12 servings

6 medium potatoes,
   cooked in jackets
1/2 cup butter or margarine
1 tsp. parsley flakes
1/4 cup onion, chopped

1 tsp. dry or prepared mustard
1/4 tsp. pepper
1/2 cup milk
1/4 cup cheese, grated

1. Dice potatoes and place in greased casserole.
2. Melt butter. Add other ingredients and heat until cheese is melted.
3. Pour sauce over potatoes and bake at 350° for 45 minutes.

Variation:
   Omit cheese. Add 1 cup sour cream, plus 1 lb. cooked, diced ham.

Sweet Potato Croquettes

sweet potatoes
bread crumbs

margarine

1. Wash potatoes thoroughly. Cook until tender. Peel potatoes while hot. Mash them immediately with electric mixer. Beat until smooth. (Potato fibers will cling to beaters.)
2. Chill mashed potatoes for several hours in refrigerator. Shape potatoes into uniform croquettes approximately 3" x 1¹/4." Roll in bread crumbs.
3. Cook croquettes in margarine, turning so all sides brown. Serve immediately.

    Croquettes may also be frozen at this point and reheated in an oven at 325° for 20 minutes.

Variation: Add 3 Tbsp. brown sugar per 2 cups mashed potatoes.

Scalloped Corn

Makes 6-8 servings

3 cups fresh, frozen,
    or canned corn
3 eggs, beaten
1 cup milk

1¹/2 tsp. salt
1/8 tsp. pepper
2 Tbsp. melted butter
buttered bread crumbs

1. Combine all ingredients except bread crumbs. Mix well. Pour into buttered 1-1¹/2 quart casserole. Sprinkle with bread crumbs.
2. Bake, uncovered, at 350° for 1¹/2 hours.

Variations:
1. Add 1 Tbsp. flour or cornstarch.
2. Add 1 Tbsp. minced onion.

Corn Fritters

Makes 12 fritters

2 cups fresh, grated corn
2 eggs, beaten
3/4 cup flour
3/4 tsp. salt

1/4 tsp. pepper
1 tsp. baking powder
oil

1. Combine corn and eggs. Sift flour with remaining ingredients and add to corn and eggs.
2. Drop corn mixture from tablespoon into thin layer of oil. Cook until golden brown on both sides, turning once.

Baked Dried Corn

Makes 4-6 servings

1 cup dried corn
3 cups milk
1/2 tsp. salt

2 Tbsp. sugar
2 eggs, beaten
2 Tbsp. butter or margarine

1. Grind corn in food grinder or blender. Combine with milk and allow to stand 1/2 hour or more.
2. Add salt, sugar, and eggs. Mix well.
3. Pour into a buttered 1-quart casserole dish. Dot with butter. Bake at 350° for 45-60 minutes, or until mixture is set.

Corn Pie

Makes 6-8 servings

pastry for a two-crust pie
1 quart corn
salt and pepper to taste

2 Tbsp. butter
milk

1. Line a casserole or deep pie pan with pastry.
2. Pour in the corn; then season with salt and pepper. Dot with butter. Add milk just to moisten, but not so much that you can see it!
3. Cover with top pastry, pinching the edges together to seal.
4. Bake at 400° for 30-40 minutes, or until the crust is browned and the corn is bubbly.

Warm Slaw

Makes 4 servings

2 Tbsp. butter
1 quart shredded cabbage
1 tsp. salt
1^1/2 cups water
5 Tbsp. sugar

1 egg, beaten
1 Tbsp. flour
^{1}/2 cup milk
2 Tbsp. vinegar

1. Melt butter in saucepan and add cabbage. Stir thoroughly; then add salt and water. Cover and cook 10 minutes.
2. In a bowl mix together sugar, egg, flour, and milk. Add to the cabbage. Cook another minute.
3. Add the vinegar and serve.

Scalloped Cabbage

Makes 4-6 servings

1 small head of cabbage
1¹/₂ cups white sauce

¹/₂ cup cheese, grated

1. Slice cabbage into thin wedges, and then steam gently over medium heat until just tender.
2. Place parboiled cabbage in a greased baking dish. Pour white sauce over (see page 34 for recipe). Cover with grated cheese.
3. Bake at 350° for 30-40 minutes.

Home-Baked Lima Beans

Makes 10-12 servings

1 lb. dry lima beans
¹/₂ lb. bacon
¹/₂ cup onion, minced
³/₄ cup celery, chopped
³/₄ cup sweet molasses
¹/₂ cup brown sugar
¹/₂ cup ketchup

1¹/₂ tsp. dry mustard
1¹/₂ tsp. salt
1¹/₂ cups cooking liquor
    or tomato juice
1¹/₂ Tbsp. Worcestershire sauce
¹/₈ tsp. pepper

1. Wash beans several times. Soak overnight, making sure they are well covered with water.
2. Parboil beans in the water in which they were soaked, adding more water if necessary. Do not allow beans to become too soft.
3. Fry bacon until crisp. Drain on paper towels. Break bacon into small pieces.
4. Cook onions and celery in bacon drippings until onions become transparent.

5. Mix together all ingredients, saving some bacon for a garnish.
6. Bake at 350° for 1¹/₂ hours or more, until beans are tender.

Fried Tomatoes

Makes 6-8 servings

3 firm, almost ripe tomatoes
1 egg, beaten
2 Tbsp. milk

1 cup cracker crumbs
¹/₄ cup shortening
salt and pepper to taste

1. Slice tomatoes into ³/₄-inch thick slices.
2. Combine egg and milk. Dip each tomato slice in egg mixture and then into cracker crumbs.
3. Melt shortening and saute coated tomato slices. Brown on both sides, turning once. Season with salt and pepper.

Tomato Sauce

1 quart canned tomatoes
   or tomato juice cocktail
3 Tbsp. flour

2-3 Tbsp. water
4 Tbsp. brown sugar

1. Heat tomatoes or juice to the boiling point.
2. Stir flour and water together to make a paste.
3. Add the paste and sugar to the hot tomatoes, stirring until the sauce thickens.

Creamed Celery

(A staple on the menu of a Lancaster County, Old Order Amish wedding)

Makes 40-50 servings

12 quarts celery,
   cut up in chunks
2 cups water
1¹/4 cups sugar
4 Tbsp. butter or margarine

2 Tbsp. salt
¹/4 cup vinegar
3 Tbsp. flour
1 cup brown sugar
1¹/2 cups cream

1. Cook celery with water, sugar, butter or margarine, and salt until soft.
2. Mix together vinegar, flour, brown sugar, and cream until smooth. Stir into celery and continue heating until well blended.

Apple Fritters

Makes 12 fritters

1 cup flour
1¹/2 tsp. baking powder
¹/2 tsp. salt
2 Tbsp. sugar

1 egg, beaten
¹/2 cup plus 1 Tbsp. milk
1¹/2 cups apples, pared and diced
oil

1. Sift dry ingredients together. Beat egg and add milk. Pour into dry ingredients and stir until batter is smooth.
2. Pare and dice apples. Add apples to batter and blend well.
3. Drop by spoonfuls into light covering of oil in heavy skillet. Cook until golden brown on both sides.

Variation:
   Core the apples and slice them in rings. Dip in batter and cook until golden brown.

Main Dishes

Chicken Roast and Gravy

(A staple on the menu of a Lancaster County, Old Order Amish wedding)
Makes 6-8 servings

1^1/$_2$ loaves homemade bread
1 lb. butter or margarine
1^1/$_2$ tsp. salt
^{1}/$_2$ tsp. pepper

1 tsp. celery seed
^{3}/$_4$ cup celery, chopped (optional)
meat from a whole chicken, stewed,
    and removed from bones

1. Crumble the bread by hand into a large mixing bowl. Melt the butter; then pour it over the bread crumbs.
2. Add the seasonings and chopped celery. Mix in the deboned chicken chunks.
3. Turn into a large roast pan and bake covered at 350° for half an hour to an hour, until heated through. Dampen with water around the edge if it begins to dry out. Stir often to prevent sticking.

Note:

    You may make a rich gravy to serve over the roast by thickening the chicken broth with flour.

Chicken Pot Pie

Makes 8 servings

1 3^1/$_2$-4 lb. chicken
4 medium-size potatoes,
   peeled and cut into chunks

1 onion, diced
salt and pepper to taste
pot pie squares

1. Cook chicken in two quarts water until it is partly tender. Then add onion and potatoes and cook until they and the chicken are completely tender. Remove meat from bones and set aside.
2. Bring broth to a boil. Drop pot pie squares into boiling broth and cook 20 minutes, or until tender. Return chicken to the broth and serve steaming hot.

Pot Pie Dough

2 eggs
2 cups flour

2-3 Tbsp. milk or cream

1. Break eggs into flour. Work together, adding milk or cream to make a soft dough.
2. Roll out dough as thin as possible and cut into 1" x 2" rectangles with a knife or pastry wheel.
3. Drop one by one into boiling broth.

Crisp Oven-Baked Chicken

1. Dip chicken pieces in evaporated milk and then in cornflake crumbs. Arrange in single layer in roast pan or casserole. Cover.
2. Bake at 350° for 1^1/$_2$ hours, or at 200° while at church on Sunday morning!

Baked Chicken Barbecue

Makes 8 servings

2 3-lb. whole chickens
1 cup ketchup
$1/4$ cup water
$1/4$ cup vinegar
$1/4$ cup butter
3 Tbsp. brown sugar

2 Tbsp. Worcestershire sauce
1 tsp. dry mustard
$1/4$ tsp. pepper
$1^1/2$ tsp. salt
juice of $1/4$ lemon
1 onion, diced

1. In a saucepan combine all ingredients except chicken. Bring to a boil and simmer for 10 minutes.
2. Spoon sauce over chickens in baking dish. Add $1/3$ cup water.
3. Bake, uncovered, at 350° for 2 hours, basting occasionally.

Variation:

Omit onion. Add $1/2$ tsp. paprika and $1/4$ tsp. hickory smoke seasoning to sauce.

Creamed Chicken

Makes 4-6 servings

2 Tbsp. butter or margarine
2 Tbsp. flour
$1/2$ tsp. salt
dash of pepper

1 tsp. minced celery leaves
1 cup milk
1 cup chicken broth
2 cups cooked, diced chicken

1. Melt butter. Add flour, salt, pepper, and celery leaves. Stir until smooth.
2. Add milk and chicken broth. Bring to a boil and boil 5 minutes, stirring constantly.
3. Add chicken and heat thoroughly.
4. Serve with waffles.

Waffles

Makes 10-12 waffles

4 eggs

2¹/₂ cups milk

³/₄ cup melted shortening

3¹/₂ cups flour

6 tsp. baking powder

1 tsp. salt

1. Combine all ingredients and beat for 1 minute.
2. Bake waffles in hot waffle iron.

Roast Turkey with Duck

25 lb. turkey

3 lb. duck

filling

1. Stuff the duck inside the turkey, or lay the duck beside the turkey in the roast pan if using a smaller turkey. Stuff both the duck and turkey with filling.
2. Rub the turkey with butter and salt. Add water to a depth of ¹/₂-1 inch. Cover and bake at 350°, allowing 20 minutes per pound of combined weight.

Filling

1 cup celery, ground

liver, gizzard, and heart from

   turkey and duck, ground

6 eggs, beaten

salt and pepper to taste

8 cups bread, cubed

1. Simmer the ground celery with the ground organ meat until tender. Add salt and pepper to the eggs.
2. Mix eggs with the bread cubes. Add the other mixture and stir until the filling is moistened.

Creamed Dried Beef

4 Tbsp. butter or margarine　**4 Tbsp. flour**
1/4 lb. dried beef, thinly sliced　**2 1/2 cups milk**

1. Melt butter in skillet. Tear dried beef into shreds and drop into butter. Stir to coat with butter and then let cook until beef browns around the edges.
2. Dust beef with flour. Let that mixture brown.
3. Add milk gradually, stirring continuously, while cooking over a low heat.
4. Cook until gravy has thickened and is smooth. Serve over baked potatoes or toast points.

Three-Layer Dinner

Makes 6-8 servings

1 1/2 lbs. hamburger　**6-8 cups potatoes, diced**
salt and pepper to taste　**salt and pepper to taste**
1/4 cup ketchup　**4 slices cheese**
1 head cabbage　**1 1/2 cups milk**

1. Brown hamburger; then season with salt and pepper. Mix in ketchup. Set aside.
2. Shred half the head of raw cabbage into a greased baking dish. Add half of raw diced potatoes. Sprinkle with salt and pepper. Add all of hamburger mixture. Cover with slices of cheese.
3. Shred remaining cabbage and sprinkle over cheese. Add remaining raw diced potatoes. Pour 1 1/2 cups milk over all. Bake at 375 for 1 1/2-2 hours.

Ham Loaf with Glaze

Makes 10-12 servings

3 lbs. ground ham loaf mix
   (¹/4 pork, ¹/2 ham, ¹/4 beef)
¹/2 cup minute tapioca
2 cups milk

1 cup bread crumbs
2 eggs
1 small onion, chopped fine
¹/2 tsp. salt

1. Mix tapioca and milk. Add bread crumbs and let mixture soak for 10 minutes.
2. Combine ham loaf mix, eggs, onion, and salt. Add milk mixture and combine thoroughly. Form into two loaves and place in loaf pans or on a cookie sheet with a turned-up edge.
3. Bake covered at 225° for 3 hours. Uncover, glaze, if desired, and bake a half hour more. Cut into ¹/2-inch thick slices for serving.

Glaze

³/4 cup unsweetened pineapple juice
³/4 cup honey
¹/2 tsp. prepared mustard

1. Cook until thickened.
2. Cool. Then spread over loaves.

Ham, Green Beans, and Potatoes

2-3 lb. ham shoulder or picnic, or 1-2 lb. ham hock
4 potatoes, peeled and cut in chunks
1 quart green beans

1. Place the ham in a roaster, add $1/2$ cup water, and cover. Bake at 350° for 1-1$1/2$ hours.
2. Add potatoes and green beans to roaster. Cover and return to oven for an additional hour of baking. Serve when meat and vegetables are tender.

Variation:

This dish can also be cooked on top of the stove. Place the ham in a heavy kettle. Add 2 inches of water and cook slowly, covered, for 1$1/2$ hours. Add potatoes and green beans and continue cooking slowly for another hour, or until the meat is tender and the potatoes are soft.

Pork and Sauerkraut

Makes 4-5 servings

2 lbs. spare ribs,	**1$3/4$ lb. can sauerkraut**
cut into 3 or 4 pieces	**3 Tbsp. brown sugar**
salt and pepper to taste	**$1/4$ cup onion, diced**
dash of sugar	**1 apple, peeled and sliced thin**
water	

1. Season the meat, then brown slowly in a heavy skillet. Add water to a depth of $1/2$-1 inch.
2. Layer sauerkraut, brown sugar, onion, and apple over meat.
3. Cover and cook slowly for one hour, or until meat is tender.

Oyster Pie

Makes 6 servings

unbaked pie shell and top crust	1 tsp. salt
1 pint oysters	1/4 tsp. black pepper
4 medium-size potatoes cut	1 Tbsp. chopped parsley
into small cubes,	1 1/2 cups milk
or 2 cups crushed crackers	oyster liquor

1. Spread half of oysters over bottom of pie shell. Top with half the potatoes, or crackers. Repeat those layers.
2. Sprinkle with seasonings and parsley.
3. Pour milk and oyster liquor over ingredients.
4. Cover with top crust and bake at 375° for 45 minutes, or until potatoes are soft (with sharp fork, jag through top crust to test) and crust is browned.

Oyster Filling

white bread, sliced	milk
butter or margarine	salt and pepper
oysters with their liquid	

1. Cut bread into 1/2 - to 3/4-inch squares, including the crusts, the day before making the filling so the bread begins to dry out. Put cubes in a dishpan and cover with a tea towel.
2. The next day, melt butter or margarine in a large sauce pan. Add bread cubes to it. Pour additional melted butter over bread. Stir mixture constantly over low heat until the bread browns, but doesn't burn.
3. Cover the bottom of a long shallow baking pan with a layer of browned bread cubes. Follow that with a layer of oysters (either

whole or cut up) that have been warmed in butter; then another layer of bread and another layer of oysters.

4. Pour oyster liquid, mixed with some milk, over the whole pan. The filling should be damp throughout, but not soggy or wet. Add more milk if it seems too dry, or more bread if it's gotten too wet. Salt and pepper to taste.

5. Bake the dish at 275°-300° until it's heated through (stir it up to check) and slightly browned on top.

Moist Bread Filling

Makes 6 servings

4 eggs	**1 tsp. salt**
2 cups milk	**1 Tbsp. parsley,**
2 quarts soft bread cubes	**chopped (optional)**
4 Tbsp. melted butter	**1 tsp. sage or**
1 tsp. onion, minced	**poultry seasoning (optional)**

1. Beat eggs. Add milk. Pour over bread cubes.
2. Combine butter and seasonings. Add to bread cubes and mix well.
3. Filling can be baked in a casserole dish at 350° for 45 minutes; or it can be used as stuffing for fowl.
4. If baking in a casserole, cover tightly for the first 30 minutes; then remove cover to allow browning during the last 15 minutes of baking.

Gravy

Makes 5 cups

4 cups beef, chicken, or ham broth
1 cup cold water
1/2 cup, plus 2 Tbsp. flour

1. Bring meat broth to a boil over medium heat.
2. Pour cold water in a jar with a lid that can be tightened.
3. Add flour to cold water in jar. Screw on lid and shake vigorously. Let set a few minutes, and then shake again until no flour lumps remain.
4. When smooth, stir into hot broth gently. Continue to stir until mixture thickens and is free of lumps.
5. When gravy reaches a simmer, remove from heat and serve over meat, potatoes, rice, or biscuits.

Beef Heart

Makes 6-8 servings

3–lb. fresh beef heart   **1 tsp. salt**
8 cups water   **3/4 tsp. black pepper**

1. Trim heart of fat and fibrous veins. Place in heavy soup pot and add water and seasonings.
2. Cover and simmer over low heat for about 2 1/2 hours, or until tender.
3. When finished, remove meat from broth and allow to cool.
4. Cut away any remaining fat or fibers. Skim broth. (See recipe above for making gravy with broth.)
5. Slice heart into 1/8"-1/4" slices. Warm, but do not cook. Spoon bread filling (page 51) into center of large platter. Lay meat slices around the edge of the platter. Serve with gravy.

Stuffed Pig Stomach (or Hog Maw)

Makes 4 servings

6 medium potatoes, peeled and diced
1 small onion, chopped
1¹/₂ lbs. bulk sausage meat
1 large, well cleaned pig stomach

1. Cook potatoes and onion together until potatoes are tender. Separate sausage meat into small pieces and add to potato mixture. Stir and cook only until sausage loses its reddish color.
2. Drain off excess liquid. Stuff mixture loosely into stomach and close all openings with skewers laced with string.
3. Place in roast pan with ¹/₂ cup water. Place remaining potato-sausage mixture that will not fit in stomach in a buttered casserole.
4. Cover roast pan containing the stomach and bake at 350° for 2-2¹/₂ hours. After first hour, prick stomach with sharp fork. Place casserole of remaining mixture in oven, uncovered, and bake only for the last 40-45 minutes of baking time.
5. When the stomach is well browned, slice it and serve along with the potato-sausage stuffing.

Note:

Overstuffing the stomach may cause it to burst while baking because the stomach shrinks considerably.

Pies

Shoo-Fly Pie
Makes 1 9" pie

Bottom Layer:
1 cup brown sugar
1 egg
1 cup light molasses
$1/2$ tsp. baking soda

$1/3$ cup boiling water
$2/3$ cup cold water
unbaked 9" pie shell

Crumbs:
2 cups flour
$2/3$ cup brown sugar

$1/3$ tsp. baking powder
$1/2$ cup shortening or lard

1. Begin with the Bottom Part by stirring the egg into 1 cup brown sugar. Add molasses. Dissolve baking soda in boiling water. Add cold water; then combine with sugar and egg mixture. Pour into an unbaked 9" pie shell.
2. Cut the flour, brown sugar, baking powder, and shortening together until crumbly. Sprinkle over Bottom Part.
3. Bake at 350° for 10 minutes. Reduce heat to 325° and bake 50 minutes longer, or until done.

Half-Moon Pies

Makes 2-2¹/₂ dozen individual pies

2 quarts dried apples
3 cups water
1¹/₂ cups sugar
1¹/₂ cups brown sugar
³/₄ tsp. cinnamon

1¹/₂ tsp. allspice
³/₄ tsp. salt
pie dough for 4 9" shells
egg

1. Boil dried apples in water until water is fully absorbed.
2. While fruit is cooking, prepare pie dough.
3. Drain apples of any excess water. Blend in sugar and spices.
4. To form individual pies, shape a piece of dough about the size of an egg into a ball. Roll out into a circle until dough is thin, yet able to hold the filling. Fold dough in half to form a crease through the center. With a pie crimper, shape half the circle of dough to form a rounded edge.
5. Put ¹/₂ cup of schnitz filling on the other half. Wet the outer edge of the dough. Fold the marked half over the half with the filling. Press edges together, cutting off ragged edges with pie crimper.
6. Brush tops of pies with beaten egg, lift onto cookie sheets, and bake at 425° until golden brown.

Pie Dough

Makes 4 9" pieshells

3 cups flour
1 tsp. salt
1¹/₄ cups lard
   or vegetable shortening

1 small egg, beaten
¹/₃ cup cold water
1 Tbsp. vinegar

1. Mix flour and salt. Cut in shortening until mixture resembles small peas.
2. Combine remaining ingredients and stir into shortening and flour until mixture forms a ball. Let stand a few minutes.
3. Roll out dough on floured board.

Apple Pie

Makes 1 9" pie

6 cups apples, peeled and sliced
3/4 cup sugar
  (vary according to
  the apples' flavor)
1/4 cup flour

1 tsp. cinnamon
3 Tbsp. water
1 9" unbaked pie shell
  with top crust

1. Pour peeled and sliced apples into unbaked pie shell. Combine the sugar, flour, cinnamon, and water. Stir until smooth; then pour over apples.
2. Cover with a top crust. Seal edges. Bake at 375° for one hour.

Snitz Pie

Makes 2 9" pies

3 heaping cups snitz
  (dried apple slices)
water
1 cup sugar

2 Tbsp. lemon juice
1/2 tsp. cinnamon (optional)
2 9" pie shells with top crusts,
  unbaked

1. Cover snitz with water and let soak over night.
2. Cook just until soft; then force through a sieve.
3. To that mixture add the sugar, lemon juice, and cinnamon, if desired.
4. Pour into two unbaked pie shells. Cover with top crusts. Seal edges.
5. Bake at 425° for 15 minutes; then at 350° for 30 minutes.

Pumpkin Pie

Makes 1 9" pie

1¹/2 cups mashed pumpkin
   or butternut squash
1 egg
¹/2 cup milk, heated
¹/2 cup cream, heated
1 Tbsp. flour
1 Tbsp. light molasses or King Syrup

³/4 cup sugar
1 tsp. cinnamon
dash of nutmeg
1 Tbsp. browned butter (page 33)
pinch of salt
1 9" unbaked pie shell

1. Combine all ingredients except crust. Pour mixture into unbaked pie shell. Sprinkle additional cinnamon and nutmeg over top of pie.
2. Bake at 450° for 15 minutes. Continue baking at 350° for 45 minutes.

Variation:

Add ¹/2 cup coconut to pie filling mixture or sprinkle coconut in bottom of pie shell before filling, or on top of filled pie before baking.

Lemon Sponge Pie

Makes 1 9" pie

1 cup sugar
2 Tbsp. butter or margarine
3 eggs, separated
3 Tbsp. flour
¹/2 tsp. salt

juice and grated rind
   of 1 lemon
1¹/2 cups hot water or milk
1 9" unbaked pie shell

1. Cream sugar and butter. Add egg yolks and beat well.
2. Add flour, salt, lemon juice and rind. Add water or milk.
3. Fold in stiffly beaten egg whites.
4. Pour into unbaked pie shell. Bake at 325° for 45-50 minutes.

Oatmeal Pie

Makes 2 8" pies

4 eggs, slightly beaten
1 cup sugar
1^1/$_2$ cups light molasses
1 cup milk
1^1/$_2$ cups dry oatmeal

1 Tbsp. melted butter
^{1}/$_4$ tsp. salt
2 tsp. vanilla
^{1}/$_2$ cup chopped nuts
2 8" unbaked pie shells

1. Combine all ingredients except crusts. Pour mixture into 2 unbaked pie shells.
2. Bake at 350° for 40-45 minutes.

Cherry Crumb Pie

Makes 1 9" pie

1^1/$_4$ cups cherry juice
1^1/$_2$ cups water
5^1/$_2$ Tbsp. minute tapioca
^{1}/$_8$ tsp. salt
^{3}/$_4$ cup sugar

^{1}/$_4$ tsp. almond extract
3 cups canned sour cherries,
    drained, with juice reserved
1 9" unbaked pie shell

1. Heat cherry juice and 1 cup water together.
2. Mix tapioca, salt, and sugar with ^{1}/$_2$ cup water until smooth. Stir slowly into hot juice and water, stirring and cooking until thickened.
3. Add almond extract. Remove from heat. Add cherries. Chill until cold. Then pour into unbaked pie shell.
4. Bake at 400° for 10-15 minutes. Reduce temperature to 350° and bake for approximately 45 more minutes.
   Add crumbs to top of pie when it has 30 minutes left to bake.

Crumbs

1/3 cup flour
1/3 cup sugar

1 1/2 tsp. cinnamon
1/4 cup butter or margarine, melted

Combine all ingredients and mix to form fine crumbs.

Raisin Pie

Makes 1 9" pie

2 cups raisins
2 cups cold water
1 1/2 cups sugar
4 Tbsp. flour
2 eggs, separated

1/4 tsp. salt
4 Tbsp. melted butter
or margarine
1 Tbsp. vinegar or lemon juice
1 9" baked pie shell

1. In saucepan combine raisins, 1 1/2 cups water and 1 cup sugar and bring to a boil.
2. Combine remaining 1/2 cup water and 1/2 cup sugar, plus flour, egg yolks, and salt. Add to raisin mixture. Cook until thickened, stirring constantly.
3. Remove from heat and add butter and vinegar or lemon juice.
4. Pour mixture into baked pie shell. Cover with whipped cream or meringue and serve.

Meringue

2 egg whites

2 Tbsp. sugar

1. Beat egg whites until stiff peaks form. Gradually add 2 Tbsp. sugar while beating.
2. Pile on top of pie and bake at 350° until golden brown, about 10 minutes.

Rhubarb Pie

Makes 1 9" pie

4¹/2 cups diced rhubarb
1¹/4 cups sugar
¹/4 tsp. salt
4¹/2 Tbsp. flour

1 Tbsp. lemon juice
2 eggs
1 9" unbaked pie shell

Crumb Topping:
3 Tbsp. flour
3 Tbsp. sugar

2 Tbsp. butter or margarine,
softened

1. Place rhubarb in unbaked pie shell.
2. Combine remaining ingredients and stir to form a smooth paste. Pour over rhubarb.
3. Combine crumb ingredients and scatter over filling.
4. Bake pie at 425° for 10 minutes; reduce temperature to 325° and bake 45 more minutes.

Variation:

Separate eggs and add only yolks to paste mixture. Beat whites with 2 Tbsp. sugar and ¹/4 tsp. cream of tartar until stiff peaks form. Instead of crumb topping, pile meringue on pie during last few minutes of baking time. Bake until meringue is lightly browned.

Grape Pie

Makes 1 9" pie

3 cups Concord grapes
¹/2-³/4 cup sugar
3 Tbsp. flour
1 Tbsp. lemon juice

1 Tbsp. butter, softened
1 9" unbaked pie shell
and top crust

1. Stem grapes, wash, drain, and squeeze from skins. Set skins aside. Simmer remaining pulp for 5 minutes.
2. Remove from heat and immediately put through food press (this will separate the seeds from the usable pulp).
3. Stir pulp and skins together. Blend in sugar and flour. Add lemon juice and butter.
4. Spoon into pie shell. Cover with top crust. Bake at 425° for 10 minutes; reduce temperature to 350° and bake an additional 30 minutes.

Variation:

1 cup flour	**¹/₄ cup melted butter**
¹/₂ cup sugar	

Mix together until crumbly. Sprinkle over pie in place of top crust.

Vanilla Pie

Makes 2 9" pies

Bottom Part:

1 cup sugar	**3 Tbsp. flour**
1 cup light molasses	**1 tsp. vanilla**
2 cups water	**2 9" unbaked pie shells**
1 egg, well beaten	

1. In saucepan, combine all filling ingredients except vanilla. Boil until thickened. Set aside to cool.
2. When mixture is cooled, stir in vanilla. Pour into unbaked pie shells.

Crumbs:

2 cups flour	**1 tsp. cream of tartar**
³/₄ cups sugar	**1 tsp. soda**
¹/₂ cup butter or margarine, softened	

1. Mix all ingredients together to form crumbs. Sprinkle over tops of pies.
2. Bake at 375° for 50-60 minutes.

Funny Cake

Makes 1 pie

Batter:

1¼ cups flour	½ cup milk
¾ cup sugar	1 tsp. vanilla
1 tsp. baking powder	1 egg
½ tsp. salt	1 unbaked pie shell
¼ cup shortening	3 Tbsp. chopped nuts

1. Sift dry ingredients together.
2. Cream shortening, and then blend in milk, vanilla, and dry ingredients. Beat for 2 minutes.
3. Add egg and beat for 1 more minute.
4. Pour into pie shell.
5. Make either the Chocolate Sauce or Butterscotch Sauce below. Pour one of those sauces while still warm over batter in pie shell.
6. Sprinkle with nuts.
7. Bake at 350° for 50-55 minutes.

Chocolate Sauce

1 square unsweetened chocolate	¼ cup butter or margarine
½ cup water	½ tsp. vanilla
⅔ cup sugar	

1. In saucepan over low heat combine chocolate and water. Stir until chocolate is melted.
2. Add sugar and stir constantly until mixture boils.
3. Remove from heat and blend in butter and vanilla.

Butterscotch Sauce

¼ cup butter or margarine	3 Tbsp. water
½ cup brown sugar	½ tsp. vanilla
2 Tbsp. light corn syrup	

1. Combine butter, brown sugar, and corn syrup in a saucepan and bring to a boil.
2. Add water and cook 1-2 minutes.
3. Remove from heat and blend in vanilla.

Mincemeat Pie

Makes 1 9" pie

**beef bone to yield
 2 cups cooked meat
1¹/₂ cups raisins
3 cups apples,
 peeled and chopped fine
¹/₂ cup brown sugar
¹/₃ cup fresh orange sections,
 cut in small pieces**

**¹/₄ cup fresh lemon sections,
 cut in small pieces
¹/₄ tsp. salt
1 tsp. cinnamon
¹/₂ tsp. cloves
¹/₃ cup cider
1 9" unbaked pie shell
 and top crust**

1. Simmer beef bone until meat is tender. Cut meat in fine pieces.
2. Combine beef with remaining ingredients and simmer 10-15 minutes (add some beef broth if needed to keep mixture from getting dry).
3. Pour into unbaked pie shell. Cover with top crust; seal edges thoroughly.
4. Bake at 425° for 15 minutes; then reduce temperature to 375° and bake another 35 minutes.

Apple Dumplings

Makes 8 servings

8 apples, cored and pared
3 cups flour
1 tsp. salt
1¹/₄ cups shortening
1 egg, beaten

¹/₃ cup cold water
1 Tbsp. vinegar
½ cup butter or margarine
1 cup brown sugar
4 Tbsp. water

1. Mix flour and salt. Cut in shortening until mixture resembles fine peas.
2. Combine egg, ¹/₃ cup cold water, and vinegar and stir into shortening mixture. Let stand a few minutes.
3. Roll out dough on a floured board and cut into squares, so that each is large enough to fit up around an apple.

   Sit an apple in the center of a square of dough. Fold the dough up over the apple so it is completely enclosed. Pinch edges of dough to keep it from opening while baking. Place in a greased 9" x 13" baking pan. Repeat with remaining apples.
4. Bring butter or margarine, brown sugar, and 4 Tbsp. water to a boil. Pour over dumplings.
5. Bake at 350° for 40-50 minutes, or until dumplings are golden brown.
6. Serve warm with milk.

Cakes & Cookies

Blueberry Cake

Makes 9-12 servings

³/4 cup sugar
¹/4 cup vegetable oil
1 egg
½ cup milk

2 cups flour
2 tsp. baking powder
¹/2 tsp. salt
2 cups blueberries, well drained

1. Cream together the sugar, oil, and egg until lemon-colored. Stir in milk, thoroughly.
2. Sift together the flour, baking powder, and salt and stir into creamed mixture.
3. Gently fold in the blueberries.
4. Spread batter into a greased and floured 9" x 9" square baking pan. Sprinkle with topping. Bake 45-50 minutes at 375°. Serve warm.

Topping

¹/4 cup butter or margarine
¹/2 cup sugar

¹/3 cup flour
¹/2 tsp. cinnamon

1. Melt butter. Stir in sugar, flour, and cinnamon.
2. Crumble over cake batter.

Banana Nut Cake

Makes 1 long cake

4 cups ripe bananas, cut fine

2 eggs, beaten

1^1/$_2$ cups sugar

^{1}/$_2$ cup oil

1 tsp. vanilla

^{1}/$_2$ cup nuts, chopped

2 cups flour

2 tsp. baking soda

1 tsp. salt

1. Cream bananas, eggs, sugar, oil, and vanilla together until smooth. Stir in nuts.
2. Sift together flour, baking soda, and salt.
3. Add dry ingredients to creamed mixture, blending just until all ingredients are moistened. Do not over-mix.
4. Bake at 350° for 40-45 minutes in a greased 9" x 13" pan.

Carrot Cake

Makes 1 long cake

3 eggs

2 cups flour, sifted

2 cups sugar

1^1/$_4$ cups vegetable oil

2 tsp. baking soda

1 tsp. cinnamon

1 tsp. salt

2 tsp. vanilla

1 cup shredded coconut

1 cup walnuts, chopped

1 cup crushed pineapple, drained

2 cups raw carrot, shredded

1. Beat eggs well; then add the next seven ingredients and beat well until smooth.
2. Stir in the coconut, nuts, pineapple, and carrots with a mixing spoon.
3. Pour into a greased 9" x 13" cake pan and bake at 350° for 50 minutes.
4. When cake is slightly warm, spread with Cream Cheese Frosting.

Cream Cheese Frosting

4 Tbsp. butter or margarine, softened **2 cups 10x sugar**
3 oz. package cream cheese, softened **1 tsp. vanilla**

1. Beat together until smooth.
2. Spread on slightly warm cake.

Spice Cake

Makes 1 layer cake or 1 long cake

2 cups brown sugar **1 tsp. cinnamon**
1/2 cup butter, softened **1 tsp. nutmeg**
2 eggs **1 tsp. baking soda**
2 1/2 cups sifted flour **1 cup sour milk**
1 1/2 tsp. baking powder **1 tsp. vanilla**

1. Cream sugar and butter together until fluffy. Add eggs and beat until light.
2. Sift together all dry ingredients, then add them alternately with the milk to the creamed mixture, beating well after each addition. Mix in the vanilla.
3. Pour into greased layer pans or a 9" x 13" cake pan. Bake at 350° for 35-40 minutes.

Variations:
    Use ground cloves instead of nutmeg.
    Add 1 tsp. ground allspice to dry ingredients.
    Add 1 tsp. ground cloves to dry ingredients.

Moist Chocolate Cake

2 cups flour, sifted
2 cups sugar
3/4 cup cocoa
2 tsp. baking soda
1 tsp. baking powder

pinch of salt
1/2 cup oil
1 cup hot coffee
1 cup milk
2 eggs

1. Mix together flour, sugar, cocoa, baking soda and powder, and salt.
2. Make a well in the center of the dry ingredients and add oil, coffee, milk, and eggs. Beat just enough to mix well. (Batter will be lumpy.)
3. Pour into a greased 9" x 13" cake pan and bake 35 minutes at 350°.
4. Spread slightly warm cake with Quick Carmel Frosting.

Quick Caramel Frosting

1/2 cup butter or margarine
1 cup brown sugar

1/4 cup milk
13/4-2 cups sifted 10x sugar

1. Melt butter in saucepan. Add brown sugar and cook over low heat two minutes, stirring constantly.
2. Add milk and continue stirring until mixture comes to a boil.
3. Remove from heat and cool. Add 10x sugar until frosting reaches spreading consistency.

Whoopie Pies

Makes 4 dozen sandwich cakes

2 cups sugar
1 cup shortening
2 eggs
4 cups flour
1 cup baking cocoa

1 tsp. salt
1 cup sour milk
2 tsp. vanilla
2 tsp. baking soda
1 cup hot water

1. Cream sugar and shortening. Add eggs.
2. Sift together flour, cocoa, and salt. Add to creamed mixture alternately with sour milk. Add vanilla.
3. Dissolve soda in hot water and add last. Mix well.
4. Drop by rounded teaspoonsful onto greased cookie sheet. Bake at 400° for 8-10 minutes.
5. Make sandwiches from 2 cookies held together with Whoopie Pie Filling.

Filling

2 egg whites, beaten	4 cups 10x sugar
4 Tbsp. milk	1^1/$_2$ cups shortening
2 tsp. vanilla	

1. Mix together egg whites, milk, vanilla, and 2 cups 10x sugar. Then beat in shortening and remaining 2 cups of 10x sugar.
2. Spread dab of filling on flat side of cooled cookie. Top with another cookie to form a sandwich pie.

Coffee Crumb Cake

Makes 1 long cake

3 cups flour	1 egg, beaten
2 cups brown sugar	1 cup buttermilk
1/2 cup shortening, butter,	1 tsp. baking soda
or margarine, softened	1 tsp. cream of tartar

1. Mix flour and brown sugar together. Cut in shortening until mixture is crumbly. Take out 1 cup crumbs for topping.
2. Add to remaining crumbs, the next 4 ingredients in the order they are listed. Mix well after each addition.
3. Pour into a greased 9" x 13" baking pan. Sprinkle reserved cup of crumbs over top. Bake at 375° for 25-30 minutes.

Oatmeal Cake

Makes 1 long cake

1¹/4 cups boiling water
1 cup oatmeal
¹/2 cup margarine, softened
1 cup brown sugar
1 cup sugar
2 eggs

1¹/2 cups flour
1 tsp. baking soda
2 tsp. baking powder
1 tsp. cinnamon
1 tsp. salt

1. Pour boiling water over oatmeal. Set aside.
2. Cream together margarine, sugars, and eggs. Then add oatmeal mixture and the remaining ingredients.
3. Pour batter into a greased 9" x 13" baking pan and bake at 350° for 30 minutes.
4. Cool cake and spread with Topping. Put under broiler until Topping bubbles, about 2 minutes. (Watch closely! The Topping can burn quickly.)

Topping

¹/4 cup butter or margarine,
   softened
²/3 cup brown sugar

¹/4 cup milk
1 cup coconut
1 cup pecans, chopped

1. Mix together and spread on cake.
2. Return cake to oven and broil 5 minutes, or until Topping bubbles and is slightly browned.

Shoo-Fly Cake

Makes 1 long cake

4 cups flour (use 2 cups whole
   wheat flour and 2 cups white
   flour, if desired)
2 cups brown sugar
1 cup butter or margarine, softened

2 cups boiling water
1 cup molasses
   (use light or sweet, not dark)
2 tsp. baking soda

1. Work the flour, sugar, and butter into fine crumbs with your fingers or a pastry mixer. Set aside $1^1/2$ cups crumbs for topping.
2. Mix water, molasses, and baking soda together. Add to the remaining crumbs. Mix until batter is very thin yet still lumpy.
3. Pour into greased and floured 9" x 13" cake pan. Sprinkle with reserved crumbs. Bake at 350° for 35 minutes.

Butter Cream Icing

Icing for 1 long cake

3 Tbsp. butter, margarine,
   or shortening
$1^1/2$ cups 10x sugar

1 Tbsp. cream or milk
$1/2$ tsp. vanilla

1. Beat shortening until smooth. Cream with sugar by hand or electric mixer.
2. When smooth, add cream or milk and vanilla, beating until creamy.

Peanut Butter Icing

1/4 cup peanut butter
1 lb. 10x sugar

1/4 tsp. vanilla
4-5 Tbsp. milk

Combine all ingredients and beat until smooth and creamy. Frost cake and serve.

Chocolate Chip Icing

5 Tbsp. margarine, softened
1 cup sugar

6-oz. pkg. chocolate chips
1/3 cup milk

1. Combine margarine, sugar, and chocolate chips in saucepan. Stir until melted over medium heat. Add milk and stir until shiny.
2. Spread warm icing over cooled cake.

Sugar Cookies

(Makes enough for a crowd!—about 18-20 dozen cookies)

4 1/2 cups brown sugar
2 cups lard, melted
2 cups sour cream
8 eggs
3 tsp. baking soda

3 tsp. cream of tartar
9 cups flour
1 Tbsp. vanilla
pinch of salt

1. Cream the sugar and lard together. Add the sour cream and eggs and beat well. Stir in the remaining ingredients and mix well.
2. Drop by teaspoonsful onto greased cookie sheets. Bake at 325° 8-10 minutes.

Soft Molasses Cookies

Makes 8 dozen cookies

1 cup shortening, softened	2 cups buttermilk
1/2 lb. light brown sugar	6 cups flour
2 cups dark baking molasses	1 Tbsp. baking soda

1. Cream shortening and sugar together. Add molasses and buttermilk.
2. Stir in flour and baking soda.
3. Drop in large dollops from teaspoon onto cookie sheet. Bake at 375° for 8-10 minutes.

Variations:

Cookies may be glazed by brushing tops with egg yolk before baking. Add 1 tsp. ginger and 1 tsp. cinnamon with flour and soda.

Snickerdoodles

Makes 4 dozen cookies

1 cup shortening, softened	1 tsp. baking soda
1 1/2 cups sugar	1/2 tsp. salt
2 eggs	2 Tbsp. sugar
2 3/4 cups flour	2 tsp. cinnamon
2 tsp. cream of tartar	

1. Cream shortening and sugar together. Add eggs and beat well.
2. Sift together flour, cream of tartar, soda, and salt. Gradually stir into creamed mixture.
3. Chill dough 2 hours or more. Form into balls the size of walnuts.
4. Roll each ball in a mixture of 2 Tbsp. sugar and 2 tsp. cinnamon. Bake at 400° for about 10 minutes. (Cookies should be lightly browned but still soft.)

Chocolate Chip Sour Cream Cookies

Makes about 8 dozen cookies

1 cup shortening, softened
2 cups sugar
4 eggs
1 cup sour cream
4 cups flour
1/2 tsp. salt

2 tsp. baking soda
12-16 oz. chocolate chips
1 cup chopped nuts
2 cups raisins, boiled, cooled,
    and drained (optional)

1. Cream shortening and sugar together.
2. Add eggs and beat till fluffy. Add sour cream and mix well.
3. Gradually add flour, salt, and soda. Mix well.
4. Stir in chocolate chips, nuts, and raisins, if desired.
5. Drop by heaping teaspoonsful onto greased cookie sheet. Bake at 375° for 10 minutes.

Date Balls

Makes 3 dozen cookies

1 cup sugar
1/2 cup butter, softened
dash of salt
1 cup chopped dates

1 egg, beaten
1 cup chopped pecans
2 cups crispy rice cereal
coconut

1. Heat first three ingredients over low heat until butter is melted.
2. Add dates and beaten egg and bring to boil. Boil 5 minutes, stirring constantly.
3. Cool. Add pecans and cereal.
4. Form balls that are 1 1/2 inches in diameter. Roll in coconut and serve or store.

Date Pinwheel Cookies

Makes 3½ dozen cookies

1 cup shortening, softened	4-4½ cups flour
2 cups brown sugar	1 tsp. salt
½ cup sugar	1 tsp. baking soda
3 eggs	1 tsp. cinnamon

1. Cream together the shortening and sugars. Add the eggs and beat until fluffy.
2. Sift the flour; then add the salt, soda, and cinnamon and sift again. Add the dry ingredients to the creamed mixture and beat until smooth. Chill dough in the refrigerator for a few hours.
3. Divide the chilled dough into two parts. Roll each ¼" thick and spread with filling.

Filling

1½ cups dates or raisins, ground	1 cup water
1 cup sugar	½ cup nuts, chopped fine

1. Combine the fruit, sugar, and water and cook until thickened, stirring constantly. Remove from heat and add the nuts. Cool and spread on the rolled dough.
2. Roll up, jelly-roll fashion, and chill thoroughly in the refrigerator.
3. Slice in rings ⅛ inch thick and place on greased cookie sheets, 1 inch apart. Bake at 375° until golden brown.

Puddings, Desserts, & Candies

Old-Fashioned Bread Pudding

Makes 10 servings

5 slices bread, at least 3 days old
1 cup raisins, optional
3 cups milk
1/3 cup sugar

pinch of salt
3 eggs, slightly beaten
1/4 tsp. cinnamon
2 Tbsp. sugar

1. Toast bread lightly, butter generously, then break into pieces about 1/4" square. Arrange in buttered 9" x 9" baking dish. Sprinkle with raisins.
2. Scald milk. Stir in sugar and salt. Pour over eggs and blend thoroughly.
3. Pour over bread and stir so bread is completely wet. Combine cinnamon and sugar and sprinkle over top.
4. Set baking dish in pan of hot water. Bake at 350° for 1 hour, or until a knife, inserted in the center of the pudding, comes out clean. Serve hot or cold.

Tapioca Pudding
Makes about 10 servings

4 cups milk	**1/2 cup sugar**
1/3 cup minute tapioca	**pinch of salt**
2 eggs, separated	**1/2 tsp. vanilla or lemon extract**

1. Combine milk and tapioca in a heavy saucepan. Cook, stirring constantly, until tapioca is clear.
2. Beat egg yolks with sugar and salt. Add 1/2 cup hot milk mixture to egg yolks. Return this to remaining hot milk. Heat again to boiling point. Boil 2 minutes, stirring constantly.
3. Remove from heat. Fold in stiffly beaten egg whites and flavoring. Pour into serving dish.

Variation:
Use 3 cups grape juice and 1 cup milk instead of 4 cups milk.

Cracker Pudding
Makes 6-8 servings

6 cups milk	**3 cups fine saltine cracker crumbs**
3 eggs, separated	**11/4 cups shredded coconut**
3/4 cup sugar	**1 tsp. vanilla**

1. Scald milk. Set aside. Beat egg yolks; then add sugar and blend.
2. Add egg mixture gradually to milk, stirring constantly. Cook for one minute; then add the cracker crumbs and coconut. Stir until mixture thickens and crumbs soften.
3. Beat egg whites until stiff. Then fold them and vanilla into pudding while it is still hot.
4. Chill and serve.

Caramel Pudding

Makes 4 servings

2 Tbsp. butter or margarine	2 Tbsp. flour
3/4 cup brown sugar	pinch of salt
1 quart milk	1/4 cup milk
2 eggs	chopped peanuts
2 Tbsp. cornstarch	

1. Melt butter or margarine in a heavy saucepan. Add brown sugar and stir until the mixture browns and caramelizes.
2. Stir in 1 quart milk and warm; then set aside.
3. Beat together eggs, cornstarch, flour, salt, and 1/4 cup milk. Add to warm milk and stir just until it reaches the boiling point.
4. Remove from heat and beat with a rotary beater. Cool; then cover top with chopped fresh peanuts before serving.

Variation:

Line serving dish with buttered graham cracker crumbs. Spoon in half the pudding. Add a layer of buttered graham cracker crumbs; then the remaining pudding. Top with whipped cream and dust with graham cracker crumbs.

Creamy Rice Pudding

Makes 10 servings

1 quart milk	1/4 tsp. salt
1/2 cup rice	2 eggs
2 Tbsp. butter or margarine	1 tsp. vanilla
1/4 cup sugar	

1. Stir together milk, rice, margarine or butter, sugar, and salt. Pour into double boiler and cook slowly for 1-1^1/$_2$ hours until rice is soft.
2. Beat the eggs. Remove 1 cup hot milk and rice from double boiler and gradually add to beaten eggs. Then add the egg mixture to the rest of the pudding. Stir in vanilla.
3. Serve either warm or cold.

Variations:
1. Add ^{1}/$_4$-^{1}/$_2$ tsp. nutmeg to rice mixture before cooking.
2. After pudding cools, fold in ^{1}/$_2$ cup crushed pineapple, or ^{1}/$_2$ cup banana slices, and 1 cup whipped cream.

Egg Custard

Makes about 7 servings

4 eggs	**1 tsp. vanilla**
^{1}/$_2$ cup sugar	**4 cups scalded milk**
^{1}/$_4$ tsp. salt	

1. Combine all ingredients in blender and mix thoroughly. Pour into custard cups.
2. Set cups in shallow baking pan and add hot water to cover all but ^{1}/$_2$" of the custard cups.
3. Bake at 475° for 5 minutes and then at 425° for 15-20 minutes, or until set. Cool before serving.

Variations:
1. Sprinkle custards with nutmeg before baking.
2. Add ^{3}/$_4$ cup shredded coconut to custards before baking.
3. Add 2 cups mashed, cooked pumpkin, ^{1}/$_2$ tsp. ginger, 1 tsp. cinnamon, ^{1}/$_2$ tsp. ground cloves, ^{1}/$_4$ tsp. nutmeg, and ^{1}/$_4$ tsp. salt to custards before baking.

Butterscotch Pudding

Makes 10 servings

2 cups brown sugar	1 quart milk
2/3 cup flour	1/2 cup butter
4 eggs	1 Tbsp. vanilla

1. Combine brown sugar and flour in a saucepan and mix well. Add eggs and mix to a paste. Gradually add cold milk and stir well to avoid lumps.
2. Bring to a boil over medium heat, stirring frequently with a wire whisk. Add butter and continue cooking, stirring constantly. When thickened, remove from heat and stir in vanilla.
3. To assure smoothness, beat briskly with whisk after removing from heat. Chill and serve.

Chocolate Cornstarch Pudding

Makes 4-6 servings

3 Tbsp. cornstarch	3 Tbsp. cocoa
1/3 cup sugar	2 cups milk
1/2 tsp. salt	1 tsp. vanilla

1. Mix dry ingredients together well.
2. In a saucepan heat 1 1/2 cups milk. Add other 1/2 cup milk to the dry ingredients and stir until smooth.
3. When milk is hot, but before a skin forms, stir in dampened dry ingredients. Stir constantly over heat until mixture thickens and comes to a gentle boil (it should not boil vigorously).
4. Remove from heat and serve either warm or cold.

Date Pudding

Makes about 18 servings

1 cup dates, chopped
1 cup boiling water
1 tsp. baking soda
1 cup sugar
1 egg, beaten
3 Tbsp. butter or margarine,
    melted

1 cup flour
1 tsp. vanilla
$1/2$ cup nuts, chopped
3 cups sweetened whipped cream
3 bananas, sliced

1. Combine dates, water, and soda. Mix well and let cool.
2. Add remaining ingredients except cream and bananas and mix well.
3. Pour batter into a greased, waxed paper-lined 9" x 13" pan. Bake at 350° for 30-40 minutes.
4. Allow cake to cool. Just before serving, break up cake into chunks. Fold in whipped cream and sliced bananas.

Rhubarb Sauce

1 qt. fresh rhubarb, sliced thin
water
$2^{1}/2$ Tbsp. minute tapioca

$3/4$ cup sugar
1 tsp. orange rind, grated
pinch of baking soda

1. Place sliced rhubarb in saucepan. Add enough water to cover half the rhubarb.
2. Add tapioca and sugar. Stir until well mixed. Let stand for half an hour.
3. Heat and cook the rhubarb until it is tender but not mushy. Stir in orange rind.
4. Remove pan from heat. Stir in baking soda. Mixture will foam, so stir gently to prevent rhubarb from overflowing the pan.
5. Chill and serve.

Rhubarb Crunch

Makes 8 servings

Crumbs:

1 cup flour, sifted
1/2 cup brown sugar,
  firmly packed
1 tsp. cinnamon

3/4 cup dry oatmeal
1/2 cup butter or margarine,
  melted
4 cups rhubarb, diced

Glaze:

1/2 cup sugar
1 Tbsp. cornstarch

1 tsp. vanilla
1 cup water

1. Mix crumbs until crumbly. Press half of them into a greased 9" x 9" baking pan.
2. Cover with diced rhubarb.
3. Combine glaze ingredients and cook until they thicken and clear.
4. Pour over rhubarb. Top with remaining crumbs.
5. Bake at 350° for one hour.
6. Serve warm plain, or with milk or ice cream.

Homemade Ice Cream

Makes 4 quarts ice cream

3 eggs, beaten
2 cups sugar
3 cups cream

2 tsp. vanilla
dash of salt
1 quart fruit, chopped

1. Mix all ingredients together thoroughly. Pour into 4-quart freezer container, adding additional fruit or cream if necessary to make container 2/3 full.
2. Turn freezer until ice cream is firm.

Peach Cobbler

Makes 12-15 servings

Fruit Filling:

2 Tbsp. cornstarch

1/4 cup brown sugar

1/4 cup honey

1/2 cup water

6 cups fresh peaches, sliced

2 Tbsp. butter or margarine

1 1/2 Tbsp. lemon juice

1. In a saucepan, mix together cornstarch, brown sugar, honey, and water. Stir until lump-free. Cook over medium heat until mixture thickens, stirring constantly.
2. Fold in peaches and boil mixture for one minute.
3. Remove from heat. Stir in butter and lemon juice until butter melts.
4. Pour into a greased 9" x 13" baking pan.

Batter:

1 cup flour

1 cup sugar

1 tsp. baking powder

1/2 tsp. salt

2 Tbsp. butter or margarine, softened

1 egg, slightly beaten

1. Stir all Batter ingredients together in a mixing bowl. Beat until smooth.
2. Drop by tablespoonsful over hot peaches.
3. Bake at 375° for 1 hour.
4. Serve warm with milk, whipped cream, or ice cream.

Crispy Caramel Corn

3 3/4 qts. popped popcorn
1 cup brown sugar
1/2 cup margarine
1/4 cup light corn syrup

1/2 tsp. salt
1/2 tsp. baking soda
1/2 tsp. vanilla

1. Pour popped popcorn into a large roasting pan.
2. Mix sugar, margarine, corn syrup, and salt in a saucepan and cook gently over medium heat, stirring constantly. When the mixture begins to boil, cook for 5 more minutes.
3. Remove syrup from heat and stir in soda and vanilla until the mixture becomes foamy. Pour syrup over popcorn, stirring to coat.
4. Bake for 1 hour at 200°, stirring every 15 minutes. Cool and crumble into small pieces.

Mints
Makes 90 mints

4 Tbsp. butter (or 3 oz.
   softened cream cheese)
3 Tbsp. sweetened
   condensed milk

1 lb. 10x sugar
1/2 tsp. mint flavoring
food coloring
sugar

1. Mash butter or cream cheese with milk. Gradually add sugar until the mixture is like stiff pie dough.
2. Work in the flavoring and the food coloring until the mixture reaches the desired shade.
3. Roll into small balls, then roll in granulated sugar.
4. Press into candy molds, and then unmold immediately. (The mints freeze well.)

Jams and Spreads

Strawberry Jam

1 quart strawberries　　　　**2 cups sugar**
2 cups sugar　　　　　　　　**2 tsp. lemon juice**

1. Stir strawberries and 2 cups sugar together. Bring to boil and simmer for 5 minutes, stirring frequently.
2. Stir in 2 more cups sugar and lemon juice. Bring to boil and continue boiling for 10 more minutes, stirring frequently.
3. Let stand for 24 hours.
4. Spoon into jars and seal.

Grape Jelly

1 lb. grapes　　　　　　　**3 Tbsp. water**
1 lb. sugar

1. Combine all ingredients. Boil for 20 minutes.
2. Put through food press.
3. Pour into jars and seal.

Old-Fashioned Peach Preserves

2 quarts peeled and sliced ripe peaches
6 cups sugar

1. Stir fruit and sugar together in a large kettle. Let stand in cool place for 12-18 hours.
2. Bring to boil, stirring often. Let simmer until fruit thickens and becomes clear, about 40 minutes. Continue to stir throughout cooking time.
3. Spoon into jars and seal.

Apple Butter in the Oven

8 quarts thick applesauce   **4 cups brown sugar**
8 quarts fresh cider   **1 tsp. salt**

1. Heat applesauce, place in large baking pan, and put into oven set at 400°.
2. Place cider in large kettle and boil until half has evaporated. Add cider to sauce in the oven. Allow oven door to stand slightly ajar so steam can escape. Stir occasionally.
3. After about 2 hours add sugar and salt. Mix well.
4. Allow about 2 more hours of cooking time, until apple butter is of desired consistency, remembering to stir occasionally.
5. Seal in jars.

Pear Honey

6 quarts pear sauce
1 quart apple cider

$1/4$ tsp. cinnamon
3 lbs. brown sugar

1. To make pear sauce, wash, core, and peel pears. Cut into quarters. Add a little water and cook until soft and mushy.
2. Mix pear sauce with cider, cinnamon, and brown sugar in large roaster. Place in a 400° oven for 3-4 hours. Stir occasionally during baking time. Allow oven door to stand a bit ajar so moisture can escape. The mixture will boil down to about half the original volume.
3. Put in jars and seal.

Church Spread

4 cups light corn syrup or molasses
4 cups marshmallow cream
$1^1/3$ lbs. peanut butter (chunky or smooth), or grape or strawberry jelly

1. Mix together well until creamy and spreadable.
2. Serve on bread or crackers.

Homemade Ketchup

Makes about 6 pints

2 pecks ripe tomatoes	2 cups vinegar
2 onions	1/4 tsp. ground cloves
5 stalks celery	1/2 tsp. allspice
2 green peppers	1/2 tsp. cinnamon
3 cups sugar	3 Tbsp. salt

1. Cook tomatoes, onions, celery, and peppers until soft and mushy.
2. Pour into colander and drain 8-10 hours.
3. Force remaining pulp through food press or strainer.
4. Place strained mixture in kettle and add remaining ingredients. Boil 10 minutes.
5. Pour into jars and seal.

Beverages

Iced Tea

Makes 8¹/₂ quarts

8 quarts water
8 bags regular tea
4 bags spearmint or peppermint tea

2 cups sugar
12 ozs. frozen lemonade
    concentrate

1. Bring 8 quarts water to boil. Remove from heat and drop in 12 teabags. Steep for 30 minutes.
2. Stir in sugar until dissolved. Add frozen lemonade, stirring until it dissolves.
3. Chill and serve.

Tea-Ade

Makes about 6 quarts

2 cups sugar (or less)
5 cups water
1 large handful garden tea

1 cup lemon juice
1 cup orange juice
water

1. Boil sugar in 5 cups water. Pour over garden tea. Cover and steep for 1 hour.
2. Remove tea. Add juices. Refrigerate.
3. To serve, dilute concentrate with 2 parts water to 1 part concentrate.

Mint Meadow Tea

Makes 1/2 gallon

1 cup sugar
1 pint water
1 cup fresh tea leaves,
    either peppermint or spearmint

juice of 1 lemon
water

1. Stir sugar and pint of water together in a saucepan and bring to a boil.
2. Pour boiling syrup over tea leaves and let steep for 20 minutes. Remove the leaves and let tea cool.
3. Add the lemon juice and enough water to make 1/2 gallon of tea.
4. Serve either hot or cold.

Fresh Lemonade

Makes 1 gallon

4 lemons
3 cups sugar

1 quart hot water
3 quarts cold water

1. Wash and slice lemons. Remove seeds. Stomp lemon slices and sugar together with a potato masher until lemon pulp and sugar are well mixed.
2. Add hot water to lemon-sugar mixture and stir until sugar is dissolved and lemon pulp and juice are extracted.
3. Squeeze lemon slices by hand to get balance of juice before disposing of slices. Add cold water to mixture and stir until well blended.
4. Chill and serve.

Quick Root Beer

Makes 1 gallon

1 tsp. dry yeast
1 cup lukewarm water
2 cups sugar

5 tsp. root beer extract
lukewarm water
6-10 raisins

1. Dissolve yeast in 1 cup lukewarm water. Let stand 5 minutes.
2. Combine sugar and extract. Add yeast mixture to it. Pour into gallon jug, then fill with lukewarm water, stopping 1 inch from the top. Add dried raisins for flavor.
3. Cover jar and set in the sun for 3 hours. Refrigerate overnight.
4. Drink the next day!

Rhubarb Punch

2 lbs. tender rhubarb
5 cups water
1/4 cup lemon juice

sugar
grapefruit juice
1 quart ginger ale

1. Chop rhubarb. Combine rhubarb with water and cook until mushy.
2. Strain well, reserving only the juice. Add lemon juice to this concentrate.
3. For each cup of concentrate add 1/3 cup sugar and 1/2 cup grapefruit juice.
4. Chill well. Just before serving, add chilled ginger ale and stir well.

Grape Juice

10 lbs. Concord grapes   **1¹/₂ lbs. sugar**
2 cups water

1. Wash grapes, add water, and cook until soft.
2. Drain through fruit press until juice stops flowing.
3. Add sugar and stir until dissolved.
4. Bring juice to a boil, then pour into jars or bottles and seal.
5. To serve, mix grape juice concentrate with an equal amount of water.

Variation:
Stir in frozen lemonade concentrate to taste just before serving.

Tomato Juice Cocktail

¹/₂ bushel tomatoes   **3 green peppers**
3 stalks celery (leaves and all)   **a little water**
3 large onions   **1 cup sugar**
6 medium carrots   **2 Tbsp. salt**

1. Cut raw vegetables into 1-inch pieces. Put all together in large
   stockpot. Add water to a depth of 1 inch. Cook slowly until
   vegetables are soft, then put through food press.
2. To pureed mixture add sugar and salt.
3. Return to stockpot and bring to a boil. Pour into canning jars and
   seal.

Index

About the Author

Phyllis Pellman Good is a *New York Times* bestselling author. A native of Lancaster County, Pennsylvania, she did not realize that the cooking traditions of her home area were distinctive until she discovered visitors intent on learning about Shoo-Fly Pie and Chicken Corn Soup.

She has since authored several cookbooks, including *The Best of Amish Cooking*. She is co-author of *The Best of Mennonite Fellowship Meals, From Amish and Mennonite Kitchens, Favorite Recipes with Herbs,* and the national bestseller *Fix-It and Forget-It Cookbook*.

Together with her husband Merle, she has co-authored the bestselling book, *20 Most Asked Questions About the Amish and Mennonites*.

The Goods are co-executive directors of The People's Place, an educational center about the Amish and Mennonites in the village of Intercourse, Pennsylvania. They also operate The Old Country Store.